# Things That I       ld

Teacher's Choice Series

**Bunny Humphrey**
Pima, Arizona

Illustrations by
Steve Pileggi

Dominie Press, Inc.

The development of the *Teacher's Choice Series* was supported by the Reading Recovery project at California State University, San Bernardino. All authors' royalties from the sale of the *Teacher's Choice Series* will be used to support various Reading Recovery projects.

Publisher: Raymond Yuen
Series Editor: Stanley L. Swartz
Illustrator: Steve Pileggi
Cover Designer: Steve Morris
Page Design: Michael Khoury

Published by:

🔲 Dominie Press, Inc.

1949 Kellogg Avenue
Carlsbad, California 92008 USA

ISBN 1-56270-576-8
Printed in Singapore by PH Productions Pte Ltd.
2 3 4 5 6 IP 99 98 97

A plow drags behind a tractor.

A trailer drags behind a truck.

A boxcar drags behind a train.

A tail drags behind a beaver.

A banner drags behind a plane.

A skier drags behind a boat.

And my wagon drags behind me.

## About the Author

Bunny Humphrey was a housewife for 22 years before turning to teaching. She has taught P.E., and now teaches Title I and Reading Recovery™ at Pima Elementary School in Pima, Arizona. Bunny and her husband, Larry, have three daughters and one son. They reside in Pima, Arizona. During the summer, she manages the town pool, and gives swimming lessons. She also coaches a swim team. She enjoys wildlife conservation, quilting, breadmaking, gardening, and illustrating.